# Adorable Animals

**Mary Quattlebaum**

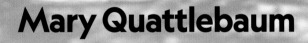

NATIONAL GEOGRAPHIC

Washington, D.C.

## To Grayson and Ben —M.Q.

Published by National Geographic Partners, LLC, Washington, DC 20036.

Designed by Anne LeongSon

**Author's Note**
The author and publisher gratefully acknowledge the literacy review of this book by Mariam Jean Dreher, professor emerita of reading education, University of Maryland, College Park, and fact-checking by Michelle Harris.

**Photo Credits**
AL=Alamy Stock Photo; AS= Adobe Stock Cover, Tony Wu/Minden Pictures; header (throughout): Lucky Creative's/AS; wectorcolor/AS; bullet_chained/AS; Happypictures/AS; 1, imageBROKER/Shutterstock; 3, grape_vein/AS; 4-5, Jay Ondreicka/Shutterstock; 6 (LO), richard-seeley/AS; 7, Kelp Grizzly Photography/Shutterstock; 7-21, Oleg/AS; 8, Paul Sutherland/National Geographic Image Collection; 9, Brian E Small/AL; 10, imageBROKER/Lilly/AL; 11, Tom Ingram/AL; 12 (UP LE), Rick & Nora Bowers/AL; 12-13 (CTR), aussieanouk/AS; 14, Bill Gozansky/AL; 15, Quentin Martinez/AL; 16, Thomas Marent/Minden Pictures; 17, rudiernst/AS; 18 (UP LE), Petr Jan Juracka/500px/Getty Images; 18 (LO LE), Megan Paine/AS; 18 (LO RT), Mike Potts/Nature Picture Library; 19 (UP LE), Linda Bestwick/AS; 19 (UP RT), Art Wolfe/Getty Images; 19 (LO), Nick Dale/AS; 20, Rob Blanken/Minden Pictures; 21, R.J. Low/Shutterstock; 22-23, Terry Whittaker/Nature Picture Library; 24, David_Slater/Getty Images; 25, Ed Brown/AS; 26-27, Shannon Hibberd/National Geographic Image Collection; 28 (UP RT), FotoRequest/AS; 28 (CTR LE), eve-genesis/AS; 28 (LO RT), ezomomonnga/Getty Images; 29 (UP), Aurore Esteban/AS; 29 (CTR LE), Aleksei Permiakov/Getty Images; 29 (CTR RT), Eric Isselée/AS; 29 (LO), Tier Und Naturfotografie J und C Sohns/Getty Images; 30 (UP), Robert Downer/Getty Images; 30 (LO), ecummings00/AS; 31 (UP), Donatas Dabravolskas/AS; 31 (CTR), Diveivanov/AS; 31 (LO), Илья Подопригоров/AS; 32 (UP LE), Amanda Guercio/Shutterstock; 32 (UP RT), Zak Zeinert/AS; 32 (CTR LE), Jonas Boernicke/Shutterstock; 32 (CTR RT), Stu Porter/AS; 32 (LO RT), NymPhoenix/Getty Images; 32 (LO LE), Werner Layer/Juniors Bildarchiv GmbH/AL

**Library of Congress Cataloging-in-Publication Data**

Names: Quattlebaum, Mary, author.
Title: Adorable animals / Mary Quattlebaum.
Description: Washington, D.C. : National Geographic Kids, 2022. | Series: National geographic readers | Audience: Ages 5-8 | Audience: Grades K-1
Identifiers: LCCN 2021047157 | ISBN 9781426372728 (paperback) | ISBN 9781426374371 (library binding) | ISBN 9781426374272 (ebook other) | ISBN 9781426374289 (ebook)
Subjects: LCSH: Animals--Juvenile literature.
Classification: LCC QL49 .Q38 2022 | DDC 590--dc23/eng/20211014
LC record available at https://lccn.loc.gov/2021047157

Printed in the United States of America
22/WOR/1

# Contents

# So Cute!

Cute animals are almost everywhere. They live in mountains and deserts. They live in rainforests, grasslands, and oceans.

The rosy maple moth looks like a fuzzy toy or a friendly space creature. It can be found in eastern North America.

They come in all colors and sizes.
Let's meet some adorable animals!

# In the Mountains

In the mountains, the pika's plump body and round ears make it look like a stuffed animal. Its fuzzy brown fur works as camouflage (KAM-uh-flahj) among the rocks. This makes it hard for predators to see the pika.

Pikas eat plants. They gather and store food all summer to prepare for the winter.

Way up high, mountain goats climb and leap. Their thick, furry coats keep them warm in the cold and wind.

Baby mountain goats are called kids. They can walk a few hours after they are born.

CRITTER
terms

**CAMOUFLAGE:** An animal's natural color or shape that blends in with its surroundings

**PREDATOR:** An animal that hunts and eats other animals

Spectacled bears are the only bears that live in South America.

This mountain bear has special markings. The circles around its eyes look like glasses. That's how the spectacled (SPEK-tuh-kuld) bear got its name.

The feathers on the head of a mountain quail look like a fancy hat. Scientists think they show what the quail is feeling. They stick straight up when the bird is watchful or scared.

When the mountain quail's head feathers lie back, it is usually relaxed.

# In the Desert

Fennec foxes live in dens that they dig in the sand.

The fennec fox stays cool in the hot desert, thanks to its big ears and furry paws. Heat leaves its body through its ears. Hair on its paws protects its feet from the burning sand.

This tiny elf owl also lives in the desert. It pokes its head out of its nest in a cactus. It looks as if it is playing peekaboo.

*Whoooooo* is this? The elf owl weighs around 1.5 ounces, about as much as seven quarters.

CRITTER **term**

**PROTECT:** To keep safe

The kangaroo rat sleeps during the day. It is active during the cool night.

In the desert, the kangaroo rat hops around on its back legs. This cute critter can also use its legs to kick an attacking snake. Then it can leap up to nine feet and escape the danger.

Big eyes help the adorable Namib (NAH-mib) sand gecko spot food when it hunts at night. It eats insects and spiders.

With its pale skin, the Namib sand gecko blends into the desert around it.

# In the Rainforest

A toucan's beak is about one-third the length of its body. The beak is strong but light.

In the rainforest, many adorable animals live in the trees. In the high branches, the toucan (TOO-kan) plucks and peels fruit with its large colorful beak.

The Wallace's flying frog is easy to spot in the rainforest. Its huge webbed feet look like big mittens! They help the frog glide through the air.

When the Wallace's flying frog lands, big sticky toe pads keep it from falling.

Squirrel monkeys live in groups. There might be 10 to 500 monkeys in one group.

Up, up, up climb the squirrel monkeys! They grip branches with their small quick hands. They scamper and leap, using their long tails to balance.

Fruit bats rest by hanging upside down.

Some people may not think bats are cute. But with its furry face and pointy ears and snout, this fruit bat looks like a friendly dog.

CRITTER
term

**SNOUT:** The part of an animal's face that sticks out and includes the mouth and nose

# 6 ADORABLE
## Facts About
## Baby Animals

**1**

After they hatch, tiny sea turtles scuttle from their sandy nest to the ocean.

**2**

A baby Nile crocodile gets a ride to the water—in its mother's mouth!

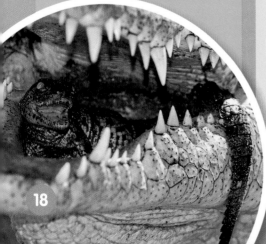

**3**

The bee hummingbird is the smallest bird in the world. Its nest is only one inch wide. This photo shows the nest's actual size.

**4**

Mallard ducklings are covered in soft feathers. They can swim about a day after they hatch.

**5**

A baby giraffe is about six feet tall when it is born. An hour after birth, it can stand on its own.

**6**

A cheetah cub is born with long yellowish gray fur down its back. Scientists think this gives it extra camouflage from predators while it is young.

# In the Grasslands

The red-tailed bumblebee flies through the grasslands. Its body is fuzzy all over. As the bee moves from flower to flower, its body hairs help spread a dust called pollen. The bee buzzes and hums while it works.

The red-tailed bumblebee is commonly found in Europe.

Wombats eat grasses and roots.

In Australia, wombats waddle adorably on their short legs and wide feet. A baby first leaves its mother's pouch when it is about five months old.

## CRITTER terms

**POUCH:** A pocketlike part of an animal's body often used to carry babies

**GRASSLAND:** A large open area of land with few trees and covered with grass

The fluffy black-footed cat walks quietly through the African grasslands. It is the smallest wild cat in Africa. An adult weighs about as much as a pet kitten.

But this wild cat is a fierce hunter. It can catch 10 to 14 small animals in one night.

The black-footed cat gets its name from the black pads and black hair on the bottom of its paws. These pads and hair protect the cat's feet from the hot ground.

# In the Ocean

The oceans are full of cute creatures! Check out this tiny bobtail squid. Most are no longer than two inches. That's about the size of two quarters laid side by side. This squid also glows, like a living flashlight.

The Hawaiian bobtail squid spends most of its time hiding in the sand. It comes out at night to hunt.

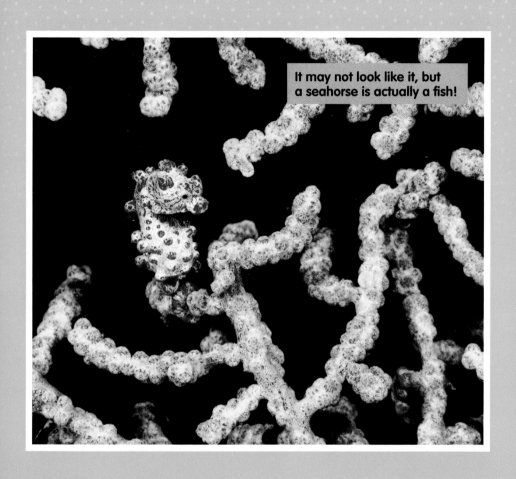

It may not look like it, but a seahorse is actually a fish!

Can you find the pygmy seahorse? Its small bumpy body looks like the coral it lives in. This makes it difficult for predators to spot it.

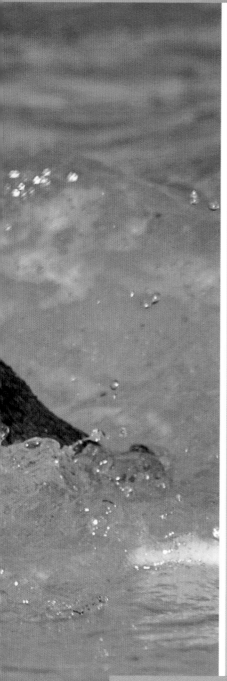

The name little penguin perfectly matches the world's smallest penguin. It is about a foot tall. In the ocean, it hunts for fish. On land, it waddles on its little pink feet. It cannot fly.

Each little penguin has its own special call. They use their calls to find one another in large groups.

27

# MORE
# Adorable Animals

There are so many adorable animals to discover! Which one is your favorite?

bee hummingbird

hedgehog

Japanese dwarf
flying squirrels

28

peach-faced
lovebirds

sea slug

cheetah cub

harp seal pup

29

# QUIZ WHIZ

How much do you know about adorable animals? After reading this book, probably a lot! Take this quiz and find out.

Answers are at the bottom of page 31.

**1** The wombat carries its baby _____.
A. with its teeth
B. on its back
C. on its head
D. in a pouch

**2** The long yellowish gray fur on the back of the cheetah cub _____.
A. looks like the fur on an adult cheetah
B. may help hide it from predators
C. attracts other cubs
D. changes color when the cub is scared

**3** Which animal makes a nest in a cactus?
A. toucan
B. little penguin
C. elf owl
D. squirrel monkey

**4** The toucan uses its large beak _____.
A. to fight predators
B. to pluck and peel fruit
C. to dig in the ground
D. to open boxes

**5** Which animal is a fish?
A. pygmy seahorse
B. green sea turtle
C. Nile crocodile
D. pika

**6** How big can a Hawaiian bobtail squid get?
A. as large as a blue whale
B. the size of a grain of salt
C. about the size of two quarters side by side
D. as long as a human leg

**7** Thick fur keeps which animal warm?
A. mountain goat
B. red-tailed bumblebee
C. mallard duckling
D. bee hummingbird

Answers: 1. D, 2. B, 3. C, 4. B, 5. A, 6. C, 7. A

# GLOSSARY

**CAMOUFLAGE:** An animal's natural color or shape that blends in with its surroundings

**GRASSLAND:** A large open area of land with few trees and covered with grass

**POUCH:** A pocketlike part of an animal's body often used to carry babies

**PREDATOR:** An animal that hunts and eats other animals

**PROTECT:** To keep safe

**SNOUT:** The part of an animal's face that sticks out and includes the mouth and nose